| square
| circle
| star
| triangle |

A companion to The Shapes Test™ book

MyShapes Journal

UNDERSTAND YOURSELF
UNDERSTAND OTHERS
MAKE YOURSELF UNDERSTOOD

PAUL CLAYTON GIBBS

MyShapes Journal: A Companion to The Shapes Test™ Book
Copyright © 2021 by Paul Clayton Gibbs

Published by Harris House Publishing
harrishousepublishing.com
Colleyville, Texas
USA

Cover creation by Ronaldo Andrade, Jr. | design by Paul Clayton Gibbs

ISBN: 978-1-946369-57-4
BISAC: SELF-HELP / Personal Growth / General

All rights reserved. No portion of this book may be reproduced, stored in a retrieval system, or transmitted in any form or by any means—electronic, mechanical, photocopy, recording, or any other—except for brief quotation in printed reviews, without the prior permission of the publisher.

The Shapes Test™ items, feedback report, training curricula, and e-learning are protected by copyright of Masterclass Suites, LLC, 2020. All rights reserved.

What people are saying about The Shapes Test™

THE SPOUSE
"Our cultures and family dynamics couldn't be more opposite! This book lets me understand my husband's frame of mind and be more supportive in his endeavors."

Alexandra Swires-Murphy | Syria | Triangle
An Arab married to an American

THE BUSINESS CEO
"Most of my time is spent navigating people's challenges. The Shapes Test™ has created a powerful tool with which to overcome them."

Matthew Powell | USA | Star
CEO of Dallas company Moroch Partners

THE RECRUITMENT MANAGER
"It's clear to me that integrating the Shapes Test™ into any hiring process will help you identify what makes a candidate tick and will unearth what motivates their talent."

Ian Peacock | England | Triangle
Hiring and Talent specialist in the innovation-led technology sector

THE SENIOR VICE PRINCIPAL
"This book is very powerful, it is more than a diagnostic test. It has helped me grasp why some staff run with an idea, whilst others question or retaliate."

Kirsty Sturdy | England | Circle
Senior Vice-Principal of a large secondary academy in England

THE PARENT OF A BLENDED FAMILY
"It helps me get the whole family moving in the same direction, and with the same language, even if family members are moving at different speeds."

Mike Sherrill | USA | Circle
Parent of seven children

THE SCHOOL CHAPLAIN
"The Shapes Test™ is beneficial as a tool to reinforce the identity of the students we work with and helps prepare them for future success and achievement."

Gary Ward | Australia | Triangle
Chaplain of Alta-1 CARE School

THE LAW STUDENT
"As a student of Law and Criminology, it is incredibly useful when advocating on someone else's behalf, forming and maintaining a level of trust with potential clients."

Daniel Jeffries |England | Triangle
Student of Law and Criminology LLB

THE NGO DIRECTOR
"The author seems to understand how different Shapes feel. If the fire in your heart and mind needs to be stirred, this excellent book is for you!"

Sakhawat Masih | Pakistan | Circle
Award-winning Director of The Servant Project, a nationwide Relief Agency

THE VOCATIONAL TRAINER
"Simple and grabbable from the outset, yet incisively far-reaching. A must-have for anyone intentionally discovering why they are here!"

Andy Flaherty | Australia | Star
Outdoor Guide and Team Building Facilitator

THE CHURCH MINISTER
"It will help staff and volunteers in our church cooperate, resolve conflict, and create solutions as we integrate these principles into our ministry."

Leonard Browning | USA | Star
Senior Pastor of The Journey Church Colorado

THE BUSINESS GRADUATE
"I'm already incorporating the language I've learned to express myself and I have noticed a significant difference in my relationships."

Isabella Scarinzi | Brasil | Square

Thank you for purchasing this journal!

By doing so you are contributing to the work of our partners across the globe as we train young people in how to build healthy relationships using The Shapes Test™.

Today, young people are struggling with issues that are being highlighted with the breakdown of the family unit and an increasingly polarized world. This leaves many young people without the help and input of a nurturing community. Many children, teens, and young adults feel alone and unable to cope with the pressures of daily life. This leads to an increase in:

Suicide.
Mental health issues.
Drug and alcohol abuse.
Relational insecurities.
Isolation.
Hopelessness.
Debilitating fear.

Our response to these problems is to work with our partners to provide mentors for young people. These mentors work alongside schools, youth agencies, faith communities, and neighborhood projects worldwide. They help young people build their confidence in who they are and their ability to relate to the world around them.

Support is raised for these projects through the sales of The Shapes Test™ book and MyShapes companion journal, the Masterclass Training events we present, and the other forms of training that The Shapes Test™ provides. The material within this book is copyrighted for that purpose and we appreciate your respect of that.

We do not believe that young people need to be victims but instead can be a positive force in our world. We believe in them and want to help them believe in themselves! Please understand that you are now part of that process and you can follow that work on our social media platforms.

Let's build something good together!

Discover your 'Shape-Weight'

Just exactly how much of a 'Square' or 'Triangle' are you?
What is the order of your other Shapes?
What percentage of each one do you possess?
You can now take the test and get answers to all these questions!

Discovering your 'Shape-Weight' will help you understand your personality type to a much greater degree and figure out why sometimes your primary Shape does not quite fit you. It will create the opportunity for greater discussions with your friends, and of course allow others to better understand who you are!

Go online to find out more at:
theshapestest.com

Get Training!

The Shapes Test™ offers fun, interactive presentations to help people build something good together. A Masterclass can be shaped to your needs in both length and content, and we have multiple formats for various settings.

Masterclasses are available for your business, organization, church, school or neighborhood event and come in various formats both in-person and online.

Go online to find out more at:
theshapestest.com

Get the book

Available in both paperback and digital versions, which may be purchased through Amazon.com
You can also purchase **bulk orders** through our shop.
Visit theshapestest.com

Why use this Journal?

The Shapes Test™ is written to increase Relational Intelligence: 'R.Q.'

Reading the book may only get you so far. You receive helpful information, but little about you may actually change. The MyShapes Journal aims to therefore increase the benefit of the book by providing you with an opportunity to progress through the three stages that are traditionally believed to turn knowledge into wisdom. It will give you the space to express yourself beyond the generic descriptions given in the book to more specific descriptions that define who you are as a unique individual. Then you will be able to better understand yourself, better understand others, and make yourself better understood.

Stage 1: Receiving

At this stage you are wise enough to take responsibility for what you listen to, watch, and read. Congratulations, you have taken the time to read The Shapes Test™ and this was a wise move. It is, however, just the first move towards greater Relational Intelligence.

You could say that stage 1 is: *To hear.*

Stage 2: Discerning

To discern is to make a decision as to what you have heard; is it good or bad, right or wrong, correct or incorrect? At this point, you either reject the information you have received or adopt and take responsibility to act upon it. The MyShapes Journal will help you do exactly that. It will give you an opportunity to decide for yourself if the descriptions and tips can, and should, be applied to your own life. You will get a chance to then choose what to leave behind and what to put into action.

We might say that stage 2 is: *To do.*

Stage 3: Repeating

The third stage of wisdom is key. Without this, there is no true wisdom. Although you have been wise enough to seek out good information, and discerning enough to use it, it has not yet become who you are. This only happens when you create habits and systems. The MyShapes Journal will assist you in that process. In doing so, you will experience a much greater benefit than simply reading the book.

We will say that stage 3 is: *To become.*

How to use this Journal

The Outcomes

The MyShapes Journal is designed with the following objectives:

- You will be able to define yourself in a simple and clear manner.
- You will develop a specific, more effective way to interact with others.
- You will create better methods to express your needs and be understood by people.
- You will learn new processes to deal with conflict, stress, misunderstanding, change, etc.
- You will set new and exciting goals for yourself.

The Guidelines

Please note that The MyShapes Journal is not an alternative to the Shapes Test™ book, but a companion book that is to be read alongside it. Therefore, to reap the greatest benefits from the journaling experience, you may want to use the following guidelines:

- Read the corresponding chapter of the book before completing each chapter of the journal.
- Re-read each description section before answering a question or completing an exercise.
- You can dip into any topic at any point; however, for best results it is recommended you work through the journal in chronological order. In this way, you will be taken on an intentional journey of self-discovery and self-expression.

Contents

1. **Crimewatch** - How can we build something good together?....13

UNDERSTAND YOURSELF

2. **Shtick** - What can I bring to our relationship?..............20

3. **Spot Bowling** - What will motivate me?......................28

4. **Top Trumps** - What could stop me?..............................36

UNDERSTAND OTHERS

5. **50 | 40 | 200** - How might others see me?..................48

6. **'X' 'Y' & 'Z'** - What's the worst that can happen?....................59

7. **Shape-Shifting** - What's the best that can happen?.................69

MAKE YOURSELF UNDERSTOOD

8. **Citizenship** - Who do I say I am?....................................84

9. **The Wisdom of a Fish** - How do I share what I need?..............95

10. **Social Reality** - How do I share what I have to give?..............104

1. Crimewatch

How can we build something good together?

RQ

Why?

Of the three questions in this chapter, which one do you find yourself asking the most and why?

Why can't we all just get along?

Why do people behave the way they do?

Why don't people understand me?

_____
_____
_____
_____
_____
_____

When was the last time you were misunderstood by someone and why do you think that happened?

_____
_____

My**Shapes** Journal

_____
_____
_____

When was the last time you misunderstood someone and what were the consequences?

_____
_____
_____
_____
_____

How?

In the book, the author shares four qualities of The Shapes Test™ that he hopes will encourage readers to use the material. They are: *Identifiable. Shareable. Applicable. Practical.*

To begin the process towards understanding yourself and what will drive your interest in this subject, first read the brief description of each one, and then list them according to what might motivate you the most:

1st . . . .

2nd . . . .

3rd . . . .

4th . . . .

Why did you choose this order?

_____
_____
_____
_____
_____

What?

If you were to gauge your 'Relational Intelligence' as outlined in the book—your ability to build good relationships with others—how much 'R.Q' do you think you have? Please mark where you would put yourself on the scale below if 10 is 'extremely low' and 100 is 'extremely high'.

Please circle:

0 - 10 - 20 - 30 - 40 - 50 - 60 - 70 - 80 - 90 - 100

In what areas of your relationships do you feel you are most successful?

Please circle:

Family | Work | Recreation | All of these | None of these

_____
_____
_____
_____
_____

MyShapes Journal

Case Scenario

Is there an area in your relationships in which you struggle when building something good with others? If so, what is that?

_____
_____
_____
_____

How and where do you hope The Shapes Test™ will grow your R.Q. in that area?

_____
_____
_____
_____

List 3 signs that you expect to notice if your R.Q. in this area improves.

1. _____

2. _____

3. _____

MyShapes Journal

1 | UNDERSTAND YOURSELF
What are my Shape's strengths, weaknesses, and potential?

2. 'Shtick'

What can I bring to our relationship?

Potential

Shapes

As well as taking The Shapes Test™ yourself, you may also want to encourage others in your life to complete it. The test is free to take and can be found at TheShapesTest.com. It can be helpful to take the test again just before starting the MyShapes Journal, but before you do, please remember the three tips given by the author:

1. Be honest. The test will only be as accurate as you are authentic.

2. Be open-minded. Don't try to force a result. No Shape is better than another.

3. Be quick. Don't overthink your answers or try to second guess the questions.

Which elements of the overview description of your Shape best fit you?

_____
_____
_____
_____
_____
_____
_____
_____

UNDERSTAND YOURSELF

Is there an element of the description you do not relate to? And if so, why?

_____

Could any anomalies be due to any of the three key reasons given in this section?

_____

Optional

Nobody is just one Shape but a mixture of all the Shapes.

If you would like some extra information about your personality, then as an option after you have taken the test, you will be given the opportunity to discover your 'Shape Weight.' This tool will reveal both the order of your Shapes and the percentage of each of them. You will find out just how 'Star' or 'Circle' you are compared to other Stars and Circles, plus which Shape you least embody! Importantly, it will also provide supplementary assistance in understanding areas of the book descriptions that do not fit your primary Shape. Knowing your Shape weight will also be beneficial for a later section of the journal.

My**Shapes** Journal

If you choose to discover your Shape weight, then take note of your results below:

My *Primary* Shape . . . . | Percentage % . . . .

My *Secondary* Shape . . . . | Percentage % . . . .

My *Third* Shape . . . . | Percentage % . . . .

My *Fourth* Shape . . . . | Percentage % . . . .

Average

In the book, the author gives a simple explanation of his worldview and how it influences his understanding of your personality and your potential. What are your thoughts on this? Do you also believe every individual is unique?

Please circle: Yes | No

If not, why not? If you do, is your reason similar to the author's worldview or different?

_____
_____
_____
_____
_____
_____

Potential

Can you see in yourself the potential ascribed to your Shape in this mini-chapter?

Please circle: Yes | No | Somewhat

If yes, why? If no, why not? If somewhat, what would you add or alter about the description?

_____
_____
_____
_____
_____

How do you already see yourself using this potential to make your world a better place?

_____
_____
_____
_____
_____

Tips

It goes without saying that stability, harmony, adaptability, and originality are not the exclusive gifts of their corresponding Shape. Neither is it true to say that any Shape is restricted to only having that one primary benefit. Although your Shape does not encapsulate all you have to give, understanding it can help you channel it. Therefore, read each 'tip' in the book and answer the corresponding questions below.

Tip #1: Find it in community.

The book advises you to ask those who know you best to fill in the test at TheShapesTest.com *as if they were you* and then compare their inventory with yours. You will also be presented with this challenge at

MyShapes Journal

the end of this chapter. In advance, however, if you had to guess the result they would get, what do you think it might be and why?

_____
_____
_____
_____
_____

Tip #2: Find it in a pattern.

First, list the positive qualities that people say you have and you hear most often.

....
....
....

Now look for a pattern. Is there something that connects all these qualities together?

If so, what would that be? Note: If you cannot see a pattern, show your list to a friend and see if they can spot one.

_____
_____
_____
_____
_____
_____
_____

UNDERSTAND YOURSELF

If you were to put that pattern into a short phrase what might that be?

".."

Tip #3: Find it in your frustrations.

What seems natural to you that you are surprised other people cannot do or understand?

_____
_____
_____
_____

According to the author's suggestion, what might this indicate about your potential?

_____
_____
_____
_____

Tip #4: Find it beyond the first place you looked for it.

Reread the description of your Shape. Did you automatically apply it to one area of your life? Now try applying it to the following areas of your life and circle the ones where you see it as most evident.

new relationships | old relationships | workplace relationships | those you lead | those you are led by | your job | your studies | your hobbies | your recreational activities | when you are working | when you are resting | when you are playing | when you are happy or sad

My**Shapes** Journal

Are there other areas of your life where you can now recognize this description of your Shape?

If so, where and when?

_____
_____
_____
_____
_____
_____

Challenge

As you apply the four tips listed above, which one, if any, revealed the most to you about a hidden potential you may have and how did it do that?

_____
_____
_____
_____
_____
_____

Why not explore the tip: 'Find it in community'? Gather a group of friends or colleagues together. Then, ask them to complete The Shapes Test™ as if they were you. Once you have done this, answer and discuss the following:

Were there any surprises? Did any of them get a different result? Discuss why they got the result they did. Discuss what their results tell you about other people's view of you. Discuss the benefits of them knowing and understanding your Shape.

3. Spot Bowling

What will motivate me?

Strengths

Goals

What good thing would you like to build with other people?

This might be something very practical like a project at work, a neighborhood campaign, a family event, etc. Or you may want to simply build a better relationship with someone or a certain group of people. Whatever it is, please state it below, and include details.

_____
_____
_____
_____
_____
_____
_____

Who would you like to build it with?

_____
_____
_____
_____

UNDERSTAND YOURSELF

To activate your potential in order to do this, read the description of your Shape's strengths and then list the three italicized words in order of how evident they are to you:

1st..............................

2nd.............................

3rd..............................

Why did you choose this order and what does it teach you about activating your potential?

_____
_____
_____
_____
_____

Can you relate to the quote contained within your Shape's description?

Please circle: Yes | No | Somewhat

Why?

_____
_____
_____
_____
_____
_____
_____

Amoral

To take the required leap of faith and pursue your goals, you may need to understand the type of motivation that will help you actually get started. However, before we look at these specific motivators, let's discover the perspective that the author suggests will strengthen them. In the book, he shared a story about his days as a Boy Scout and what it taught him. After reading it, is there anything that might be described as your 'Arts and Crafts badge'? A strength that you have previously seen as something to gain from personally, but may actually be more rewarding if you used it for the sake of others?

_____
_____
_____
_____
_____

As the author says:

> "Your character is the pivot on which your personality turns towards good or ill."

Personality is amoral. It is neither good nor bad; it just is. Having a shy personality does not make you a bad person or a good person. Neither does the fact that you are either talkative or thoughtful, nor that you are emotionally or logically driven. However, if something can be seen as being good or evil, it can be seen as a character trait, i.e.: kindness, faithfulness, courage, deceitfulness, greediness, etc. If your talents and strengths are what you do, and your personality describes how you do it, then it is your character that determines why you do it. With this in mind, what does the reason you use your talents and strengths reveal about your true character?

_____
_____
_____
_____
_____
_____
_____

Are there any ways in which you want to develop your character? List them below.

_____
_____
_____
_____
_____
_____
_____

Motivators

Growing in character traits such as humility, generosity, and selflessness will encourage you to use your strengths in order to make the world a better place. However, a little extra help doesn't hurt. We do not live in an ideal world, so, nurturing the specific motivators that help you reach our goals is also necessary.

List the three motivators in order of what inspires you the most:

1st............................

2nd...........................

3rd............................

MyShapes Journal

What have you achieved because you were motivated by your number one strength?

_____
_____
_____
_____

Can you relate to the quote contained within your Shape's description?

Please circle: Yes | No | Somewhat

Why?

_____
_____
_____
_____

Does the "At the end of it all..." statement summarize what you like to hear? If not or just nearly, how would you rephrase it?

_____
_____
_____
_____
_____
_____

UNDERSTAND YOURSELF

Tips

At the beginning of this chapter you set a goal by writing what good thing you would like to build with other people. In order to set goals that help you rather than hinder you, first read the tips section of this chapter in The Shapes Test™. This will act as a filter to help you improve your goal-setting abilities.

Tip #1: Set goals that are tangible.

Can your goal be measured? If so, how? If not, how might you reframe or rephrase it?

_____
_____
_____
_____
_____

Tip #2: Set goals that are within your control.

Are you in control of the outcome? If so, how? If not, how might you reframe or rephrase your goal?

_____
_____
_____
_____
_____
_____
_____
_____

Tip #3: Set goals with the end in mind.

Is it a next step to who you want to become? If so, how? If not, how might you reframe or rephrase it?

_____
_____
_____
_____
_____

Tip #4: Set goals that set out your stall.

Is it easy for you to share your goals in a simple phrase or sentence for the purpose mentioned in this section of the book? If so, write it below. If not, how might you rephrase it?

_____
_____
_____
_____
_____

Challenge

How does this chapter help you understand your strengths better?

_____
_____
_____
_____

UNDERSTAND YOURSELF

Is there an area of your potential strengths that you are currently under-using in your relationships with others? Maybe in a team you are on? If so, when thinking through your personality's strengths, what percentage of your Shape's strengths would you say you are using?

. . . . %

If you could increase that percentage, how much of your potential strength would you hope to be using in that team six months from today?

. . . . %

Now, write out your personal goals for the short and long-term to help you fulfill your potential. Include the tips, given in this chapter, which you need to apply in order to help you reach it.

Short-term

_____
_____
_____
_____
_____

Long-term

_____
_____
_____
_____
_____

4. Top Trumps

What could stop me?

Weaknesses

Pot

What obstacles do you see in your way of building something good with others?

_____
_____
_____
_____
_____
_____

Do any of these obstacles pertain to your own personality?

Please circle: Yes | No | Possibly

Do you feel you have been ignoring these obstacles or attempting to tackle them?

_____
_____
_____
_____
_____
_____

UNDERSTAND YOURSELF

Every Shape is a potential building block in the Jenga of life. If you pull out, we miss out. If I pull out, you miss out. If too many of us withdraw ourselves, we all fall down. In the book, the author shares a story of three homeless men and makes the comment that we are all tempted to hold something back, even "picking up our ball and leaving the field." Is this something you can relate to?

Please circle: Yes | No | Somewhat | Maybe in the past

In the story, the homeless men think to themselves: *"If I only pretend to throw my carrot into the stew and instead keep it to myself, who will really notice?"* What would be your carrot? The thing you have most frequently thought no one will notice about you if you don't contribute it?

_____
_____
_____
_____
_____
_____

Isolators

The book lists the primary way that each Shape may isolate both themselves and their gifts. As difficult as this might be to read, it may help you acknowledge, battle, and confront your behavior when you see the signs of your 'isolator' approaching. Therefore, take a look at the description of how your Shape may do this and answer the following questions:

Do you agree with the isolator listed for your Shape?

Please circle: Yes | No | Somewhat | Maybe in the past

Why is this?

_____
_____
_____
_____

Our desire to withdraw may at times be overridden by our maturity and good character. In the surveys, people often talked about the ways they had begun to overcome their weaknesses. Do you feel you have learned self-discipline when tempted to isolate yourself or withdraw what you have to contribute? If so, how has this changed your relationships?

_____
_____
_____
_____
_____

Two caveats are listed at the end of this section. Once you have read them, please list a time when you felt you were justified to react the way you did. Would or could you react differently today? And if so, is this influenced in any way by your understanding of your Shape?

_____
_____
_____

UNDERSTAND YOURSELF

_____
_____
_____

Environment

When reading the story of the old man leaning over the fence. Which of the two visitors do you most relate to and why?

_____
_____
_____
_____
_____

No matter where you go, you take you with you. Constantly moving in the hope that people will be different is not the answer. Therefore, to shape our world rather than withdraw from it, we have to proactively take responsibility for our environment rather than handing that responsibility over to others.

What are the 'environmental issues' that you think you may need to take responsibility for in your own life rather than hoping they just resolve themselves?

_____
_____
_____
_____
_____
_____

My**Shapes** Journal

Demotivators

List the three demotivators in order of what discourages you the most:

1st ....

2nd ....

3rd ....

Can you relate to the quote contained within your Shape's description?

Please circle: Yes | No | Somewhat

Why?

_____
_____
_____
_____
_____

Does the catchphrase at the end of your Shape's description sound familiar? Have you ever said this or something like it?

Please circle: Yes | No | Nearly

_____
_____
_____
_____
_____

Tips

The book states that to mature, we must let go of certain rights and instead take up our responsibilities. In this way, the catchphrases of our past may be replaced by new ones. You are encouraged to take responsibility for the elements of your environment you can control. Therefore, please spend a little time thinking through how the tips below might help you.

Tip #1: Set tripwires.

What early warning signs could you put in place to recognize when your 'isolator' is approaching?

___

Tip #2: Play Top Trumps.

What cards do you hold, and how can you best put them into play?

___

My**Shapes** Journal

Tip #3: Plan a route.

Looking ahead for possible problems is counterproductive of course, unless you do it to help you prepare a workaround. Planning an alternative route in advance that steers you away from the potential problem is a great way to make sure that, when you hear your catch-phrases, they don't have to lead to failure.

What obstacles might lie in the way of you getting there?

___

___

___

___

___

What could trip you up?

___

___

___

___

___

What might cause us to slow down?

___

___

___

___

___

Tip #4: Develop a support system.

How could you cancel out a weakness by using one of your strengths?

_____

_____

_____

_____

_____

Or use a motivator to overrule a demotivator?

_____

_____

_____

_____

_____

Challenge

Earlier in this chapter a paraphrase is given of a man whose character, and relationships, changed dramatically. It suggests how you can take responsibility for your environment:

> "Surround yourself with <u>a great group of people</u> who can encourage you in <u>your strengths</u>. Throw off <u>everything</u> that hinders you and <u>the negativities</u> that so easily entangle you. And run with perseverance the journey marked out for you."

To learn from this advice, first remind yourself of the goals you created in the previous chapter, then paraphrase the paraphrase! Rewrite the three sentences above, replacing the general advice that is underlined with more specific details that relate to your own life.

MyShapes Journal

For example, replace "a great group of people" with the names of people you should surround yourself with.

Please write your paraphrase below:

_____
_____
_____
_____
_____
_____

MyShapes Journal

2 | UNDERSTAND OTHERS
How can I collaborate with other Shapes and resolve conflict?

5. 50 | 40 | 200

How might others see me?

Perspectives

Numbers

How many people would you say you really trust?

Please circle:

0   1-5   6-10   11-20   21-50   51-100   100+

Based on the descriptions in the book, how many people would you estimate you have a relationship with at the level outlined in the book?

Casual Friends ___

Real Friends ___

Close Friends ___

Describe a situation where you worked though a relationship beyond the 'veneer stage'.

_____
_____
_____
_____
_____
_____
_____

UNDERSTAND OTHERS

After reading this section, would you say you have ever given up on a relationship too soon because it appeared to be going wrong, when actually it may have been going right?

Please circle:

Yes | No | Perhaps

If so, what happened?

_____
_____
_____
_____
_____
_____

Cartoons

Did you guess the Shapes of all four cartoon characters correctly?

Please circle: Yes | No | Some

How would you describe your understanding of the other personality Shapes?

Please circle: Poor | Okay | Good | Excellent

Which personality type do you feel you struggle with the most?

Please circle: Square | Circle | Star | Triangle | None

Why?

_____
_____
_____
_____

Tunnel

After sharing the humorous story of four people on a train, the author says:

> "When we have tunnel vision, we can focus on a personality trait that catches our attention but may not have a broad enough perspective to see the full person. . . . The reality is that we rarely see people the way they see themselves. In particular, we miss their intentions . . . and that is problematic."

Have you ever misinterpreted the 'why' behind what a person did? If so when?

_____
_____
_____
_____

What were the consequences of this?

_____
_____
_____
_____

UNDERSTAND OTHERS

Before the next section where you answer questions about the two potential perspectives of each Shape, please take note of the author's caveats. He points out that these are generic descriptions of the four personality types, so don't take this personality test too personally. He also mentions that not all of these negative perspectives are necessarily true of you nor are all of the positive ones.

List which attributes you relate to from the 'positive' descriptions of your Shape.

___

Which ones do you hope people would say about you?

___

Which of these have been used to describe you?

___

Now list the attributes you may also relate to from the 'negative' descriptions of your Shape.

_____
_____
_____
_____
_____

Are there any that you feel people might say of you? If so, which ones?

_____
_____
_____
_____
_____

Have you ever actually had people say any of these to you? If so, which ones?

_____
_____
_____
_____
_____

The author states that the sign of maturity is the ability to put ourselves in the place of someone else and gain their perspective. The challenge of maturity is that, once we have done this, we need to be willing and able to shape the way we relate to them. People are free to interpret our behavior however they want to, and we, in turn, are free to interpret theirs. Therefore, reflecting on how it made you feel when you read your Shape's second paragraph, would you want people to rethink their perspective toward you? And if so, how?

_____
_____
_____
_____
_____
_____

How or when should you rethink your perspective towards others?

_____
_____
_____
_____
_____

Tips

The intention of the author is to encourage us to persevere through the veneer stage of our relationships and not be dissuaded by our initial prejudices.

> "Yes, we are all flawed. Yes, we are not perfect, not a single one of us. But I must not allow my prejudgment of someone's singular action to color all of their actions. I must not start to see everything they do as either good or bad. This will lead me down the path of polarization."

My**Shapes** Journal

With that aim in mind, please read through the practical suggestions in this chapter and then answer the questions below.

Tip #1: Don't project your motives onto them.

Can you remember a time when you projected your motives onto someone?

_____
_____
_____
_____
_____

What might you do differently in the future?

_____
_____
_____
_____
_____

If you had used the suggested phrase that the author gives, how might you have said it in the situation you have written about? Please edit or paraphrase it below:

> "Hey, I noticed you did/said this _____. I'm sure you had a good reason. Would you please tell me your reason for doing/saying it?"

_____
_____

UNDERSTAND OTHERS

Tip #2: Don't believe the spin.

Do you suspect that others have put a spin on the things they told you about someone else? If so, how did you respond to that?

How might you respond differently in the future?

When would have been a good time to have used the suggested phrase? Please edit or paraphrase it below:

"Hey, I was told you did/said this _____.
I'm just wondering if that is true or they misread what you meant. Would you mind telling me if you did so/say it and, if so, why?"

MyShapes Journal

_____
_____
_____

Tip #3: Don't act before the fact.

Has there been a time when a relationship was damaged because you acted without knowing all the facts?

Yes | No | Cannot remember

If so, what happened?

_____
_____
_____
_____
_____

What might you do differently in the future to prevent this from happening again?

_____
_____
_____
_____
_____

Tip #4: Do nurture a positive suspicion.

UNDERSTAND OTHERS

Rate your yourself:

I allow my judgment of someone's *singular* action to color my view of *all* of their actions.

Always | Often | Occasionally | Rarely | Never

Why do you think that is?

_____
_____
_____
_____
_____

Challenge

If you are completing the journal on your own, how does this chapter help you understand others better?

_____
_____
_____
_____
_____

Now, thinking about your various relationships, choose one person with whom you would like to move either from *Casual* friends to Real friends or from *Real* friends to *Close* friends? NB: It could also be a colleague or family member. Then decide which tip in this chapter might best help you get through the 'veneer stage' or resolve an issue that exists between you, and then act upon it.

My**Shapes** Journal

Write down their name and the first thing you need to do to get this process moving here:

_____

_____

_____

_____

_____

Now list your short and long-term goals for this relationship.

_____

_____

_____

_____

_____

6. 'X' 'Y' & 'Z'

What's the worst that can happen?

Conflict

Polarization

In this section, the author gives examples of 'group polarization' and the issue it creates in our ability to build something good together. He also shares personal experiences with polarization as well as those of a friend. Have you ever experienced or observed 'Group Polarization' as described in the book?

Please circle: Yes | No | Somewhat

If so, how?

_____
_____
_____
_____
_____

Have you ever wondered why something you said or did upset people?

Please circle: Never | Rarely | Occasionally | Often | Constantly

If yes, did the different perspectives outlined in the previous chapter explain the reason for this?

Please circle: Yes | No | Partly

MyShapes Journal

If yes, how? If no, why not? If partly, what's missing?

_____

_____

_____

Sparks

Conflict is more easily resolved when you understand what caused it in the first place.

> "The issue of saying or doing 'X' and then being labelled 'Y' and 'Z' is not the only thing in relationships that I find frustrating. Perhaps more troubling is this: what I may find aggravating, you might not. And vice versa."

When reading the Shape's 'conflict creators', can you relate to what the book says will upset, annoy, or create conflict within you?

Please circle: Yes | No | Somewhat

If so, can you give an example of this?

_____

_____

_____

_____

Can you relate to the quote listed in your Shape's description?

Please circle: Yes | No | Somewhat

Why is this?

_____
_____
_____
_____
_____

Does the "For a . . ." statement summarize what is important to you?

Please circle: Yes | No | Almost

If yes, how? If no, why not? If almost, how would you rephrase it?

_____
_____
_____
_____
_____

Gremlins

After referencing Donald O. Clifton's comments on the film, *Gremlins*, the author states:

> "It seems to me that our weaknesses form a key part of what is lovable about us. Perhaps a friend is a little ditsy or forgetful, maybe a family member can get a tad sulky or moody. In the right quantities and at the right time, these vulnerabilities and foibles can actually draw us closer to one another. However, like gremlins who turn nasty when they are splashed with water, so our weaknesses can turn problematic when we seek to build with others. . . . When relationships go beyond passive companionship

> to proactive collaboration, what once made someone lovable can now make them loathable. . . . Before we learn how to tackle each other's gremlins in a way that does not add fuel to the fire, let's try to understand how the different Shapes react to conflict and also recognize the typical reasons they might use to explain their response."

Does the test have it right? Are you likely to react to conflict the way it predicts your Shape will?

Please circle: Yes | No | Somewhat

If yes, why? If no, why not? If somewhat, how would you add or alter the description?

_____
_____
_____
_____
_____

How do you think that affects those around you?

_____
_____
_____

How do you believe your reaction to conflict affects your reputation?

_____
_____

UNDERSTAND OTHERS

_____
_____
_____

What worries you most about dealing with conflict?

_____
_____
_____
_____

Tips

A key to resolving conflict with others is outlined in the book with this simple phrase:

> "Stop *trying* and start *training.*"

The author states that conflict is inevitable but we can prepare for it by building a better environment in which your conflicts can be resolved, sometimes before they even arise. In this way, when things get tetchy, rather than getting caught up in the moment trying to figure out what to do, you will have principles and practices already in place that can spring into action and take effect. So, please read through the tips provided in this chapter and then answer the questions in the journal below.

Tip #1: Build a bridge.

How do you feel about 'building a bridge' in which to challenge people and be challenged by them?

_____
_____

MyShapes Journal

_____
_____
_____

Tip #2: Build a vulnerable environment.

What three weaknesses do you have that you are willing to share with people?

1. _____

2. _____

3. _____

Tip #3: Build an appropriate environment.

Think of one person you have an issue with.

What is it about them that would be unreasonable for you to challenge them with?

_____
_____
_____
_____
_____

What is it about them that it would be fair for you to challenge them about?

_____
_____
_____

UNDERSTAND OTHERS

_____
_____
_____
_____

What is the difference?

_____
_____
_____
_____
_____

Tip #4: Build a forgiving environment.

Read the following and rate yourself on a scale of 1 to 5 with 1 being poor and 5 being great.

"I set a gracious tone and do not change it based upon the response I get."

I rate myself: ....

"I make sure I don't avoid a person after a disagreement."

I rate myself: ....

"I watch my facial expressions and body language so it matches my tone when being gracious."

I rate myself: ....

"I praise others in public but challenge them in private."

I rate myself: ....

My**Shapes** Journal

Tip #5: Build a listening environment.

As you read this section in the book, how do you feel you could improve your listening skills?

_____
_____
_____
_____
_____

Challenge

How does this chapter better help you understand what causes conflict between you and other people?

_____
_____
_____
_____
_____

Who do you find yourself in conflict with most? Would knowing their Shape help you understand why? What Shape do you guess they are?

_____
_____
_____
_____

As the author notes, the various Shapes' conflict creators can appear to be in stark contrast to one another.

> "... A Circle might say that a person should always come before a program, a Triangle might argue that an individual should never come before the good of a system that will benefit far more people in the long run. In a similar way, if a Star wants to suddenly change course because they feel something is not working, a Square may say it is too soon to decide, a commitment is a commitment, and they should just pull up their socks and stick with it ... at least for the time being."

Therefore, please list three people you know with whom you have conflict on a regular basis. Now ask them to take The Shapes Test™ and share their results with you. Once you have done this, think through how the description of their Shape's conflict creator helps you make more sense of what annoys, upsets, or creates conflict within them.

Name - _____   Shape - _____

_____
_____
_____
_____

Name - _____   Shape - _____

_____
_____
_____
_____

My**Shapes** Journal

Name - _____ Shape - _____

_____
_____
_____
_____

7. Shape-Shifting

What's the best that can happen?

Collaboration

Dimples

The book describes our potential as dented in the following way:

> "None of us are the finished product. I have come to realize that there is more to me than I originally thought. However, left to my own devices and without the input of others, my potential to build something good with others has 'dimples.' I believe the same is true of you. The blows of life and a lack of opportunity can limit our view of ourselves and make us feel like failures in areas where, in actual fact, we may have the ability to do something special."

Using the graphic below, The Shapes Test™ notes that human beings are designed to be interdependent, not independent, and those dimples represent areas where other people can 'build us out'.

Every Shape has potential to bring or build something out in us that would otherwise lay untapped. Take a look at the description of each Shape in this corresponding part of the book, and use the space below to note a person's name who fits that description and how they might help you in areas you want to grow.

My**Shapes** Journal

Who do you know that is a Square, and in what way might they be able to build your potential?

Name - _____

_____
_____
_____
_____

Who do you know that is a Circle, and in what way might they be able to build your potential?

Name - _____

_____
_____
_____
_____

Who do you know that is a Star, and in what way might they be able to build your potential?

Name - _____

_____
_____
_____
_____

UNDERSTAND OTHERS

Who do you know that is a Triangle, and in what way might they be able to build your potential?

Name - _____

_____
_____
_____
_____

Spheres

In the book, the author explains that the most authentic way to discover who you are is not on a mountain top, but among friends, family, and those with whom you do life. Take a look at the definitions for the three types of potential. Then, rather than guessing yourself, ask your friends and colleagues for answers to the following and make a note of them here:

What is my *evident* potential?

_____
_____
_____
_____

What is my *latent* potential?

_____
_____
_____
_____

MyShapes Journal

_____
_____
_____

What is my *absent* potential?

_____
_____
_____
_____
_____

The book outlines the three steps in which our friends, family, and colleagues can draw out our *latent* potential. Please grade yourself as to how good you are at giving people permission in the following steps.

First: People notice your potential and you take it on board.

Never | Rarely | Occasionally | Often | Constantly

Second: People give you new opportunities to explore your latent potential and you take them.

Never | Rarely | Occasionally | Often | Constantly

Third: People criticize your efforts, showing you how to improve, and you respond positively.

Never | Rarely | Occasionally | Often | Constantly

After refamiliarizing yourself with the following diagram, ask yourself: Who is it that I want to influence me most? Then, fill in the various spaces and decide how much space you need to give them in your life.

UNDERSTAND OTHERS

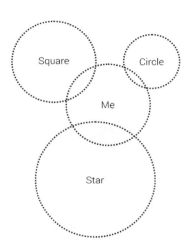

Who are you giving too little space to?

_____
_____
_____
_____
_____

Who are you giving too much space to?

_____
_____
_____
_____
_____

Please remember the author's advice here when allowing other people to influence you:

> "You may want to give them an invitation and permission to bring that influence to an even greater degree. When you do, here's what to remember: You want to learn from them but not become them!"

Now, using the simple diagram below as a reminder of this, note what you need to 'absorb' and learn from the people you have listed. Also, note the attributes you should only admire about them without feeling pressure to become like them.

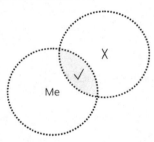

What can you absorb from these people?

_____
_____
_____
_____

What should you only admire about these people?

_____
_____
_____
_____

Change

Do you suspect your Shape will change or has it already?

Please circle: Yes | No | I'm unsure

If so, why and how?

_____
_____
_____
_____
_____

Are any of these changes due to areas in your life in which you have grown?

Please circle: Yes | No | Somewhat

Remind yourself of ways you have grown and who has helped you in these areas.

_____
_____
_____
_____
_____

In this chapter, the book explains how collaboration requires you to be changed by the positive influence of others as they *'get the best out of you.'* Therefore, once you know whose influence you wish to increase and decrease in your life, you have to face a more challenging question: What's stopping you from changing?

Do you react to change in the way your Shape is described as reacting to change?

Please circle: Yes | No | Somewhat

If so, why? If not, why not? If somewhat, what is different about your response to change?

_____

_____

_____

_____

_____

_____

Tips

Change is inevitable. Change is healthy. Change is good!

We cannot choose *if* we change, only *how* we change. Therefore, keeping an open mind is commonly understood to be a good thing. Change will always involve growing pains, but it is worth it. Your Shape is meant to help you understand yourself better, but if you allow yourself to be restricted by it in any way, that would be a tragedy. With that in mind, please take note of the generic boxes to avoid putting yourself in and answer the following questions:

Tip #1: The 'Time' Box

Are you good at giving people time to catch up with any changes you have made?

Please circle: Yes | No | Somewhat

UNDERSTAND OTHERS

If so, why? If not, why not? If somewhat, where are you weak and strong at this?

_____
_____
_____
_____

How might you improve the way you do this?

_____
_____
_____
_____

Tip #2: The 'Identity' Box

Do you feel you limit yourself and who you can be, according to your personality type?

Please circle: Yes | No | Somewhat

Why?

_____
_____
_____
_____
_____

Tip #3: The 'Behavior' Box

Do you use your Shape as a 'get-out-of-jail-free card' for behavior you want to avoid addressing?

Please circle: Yes | No | Sometimes

If so, why? If not, why not? If sometimes, when do you mainly do this?

_____
_____
_____
_____
_____

How might you avoid doing this?

_____
_____
_____
_____

Challenge

How does this chapter help you better understand your ability to allow others to bring out the best in you?

_____
_____
_____
_____

UNDERSTAND OTHERS

The Shapes Test™ proposes that we should all work towards building something good with others and that, if you can shape the way you challenge others, you can be part of the process in which someone grows into their true potential. Are you prepared to do this?

Please circle: Yes | No

Create your own Spheres Diagram similar to the one in the book. Put it in a place where it can be a visible reminder. Approach at least one person in your diagram and use the space below to determine what you say to them when requesting their help.

When you say, "This is what I can only admire about you," what will you tell them?

_____
_____
_____
_____
_____
_____

When you tell them, "This is what I would like you to teach me," what will you say to them?

_____
_____
_____
_____
_____
_____

MyShapes Journal

When you ask, "Is there anything you feel you can learn from me?", what do you expect them to suggest?

_____
_____
_____
_____

MyShapes Journal

3 | MAKE YOURSELF UNDERSTOOD
How can I express myself better and influence my world?

MyShapes Journal

8. Citizenship

Who do I say I am?

Definition

Awareness

On a scale of 1 to 10, how would you grade your level of self-awareness?

1 | 2 | 3 | 4 | 5 | 6 | 7 | 8 | 9 | 10

Without using the Shape's language, how would you normally describe yourself to people?

_____
_____
_____
_____
_____
_____

How would you like people to describe you to others?

_____
_____
_____
_____
_____
_____

MAKE YOURSELF UNDERSTOOD

In the book, the author shares a story about how he learned of the power of definition. He then explains that there are two key benefits of being able to clearly define yourself to others.

1. It warns people of what they should not expect of you.

_____
_____
_____
_____
_____

2. It holds you accountable for what they should expect of you.

_____
_____
_____
_____
_____

Do you see each of these as benefits, and if so, how might your definition of yourself help you in your life and relationships?

_____
_____
_____
_____
_____

My**Shapes** Journal

Passport

In this section, the first pathway to self-discovery is simply stated as: 'What you see yourself do.' This comes by paying attention to the fruit of your actions. As an example of this, the book suggests that a party provides a 'blank sheet' to notice your behavior, allowing you the freedom to be who you truly are. As definition comes by distinction, please read your Shape's description in this chapter, noticing how you behave differently from others. Then, answer the following questions:

How accurate is the description of your personality at a party? Does the book have it right? Are you likely to act the way it suggests your Shape will?

Please circle: Yes | No | Somewhat

If yes, why? If no, why not? If somewhat, how would you add to or alter the description?

_____
_____
_____
_____
_____

Which of the thoughts listed for your Shape at a party are most true of you?

_____
_____
_____
_____
_____

Can you relate to the quote contained within this description?

Please circle: Yes | No

If yes, why? If no, why not?

_____
_____
_____
_____
_____

After the story of how the author was given the opportunity to change his name, and why he declined to do so, he gives the following advice:

> " . . . If our behavior is in line with what we say about ourselves, people will know what they can depend upon and what they cannot. This can result in the building of trust as people acknowledge our weaknesses, but look to engage with us in our strengths. Ultimately, definition comes by doing."

Do you agree with his statement?

Please circle: Yes | No

If yes, why? If no, why not?

_____
_____
_____
_____
_____
_____

Feedback

The second path to self-awareness is noticing what people say about you.

Occasionally, people can be a little surprised when they share their Shapes Test™ results with their friends and colleagues. Often the feedback they get is that the descriptions are more accurate than they had realized because sometimes other people know us better than we know ourselves.

When you shared your test results with others, what was their general response?

_____
_____
_____
_____

Remember, if you feel that their answer encapsulates what you believe to be true, the author encourages you to thank people for their words and, by doing so, reinforce their definition of you in their minds.

Have you done this yet?

Please circle: Yes | No

If yes, what benefits have you seen? If not, do you plan to? And with whom?

_____
_____
_____
_____

This portion of the book contains suggestions of language that might help you in this process. First it states: "You will likely be appreciated for your _____." Have people given you feedback similar to the word suggested for your Shape?

Please circle: Yes | No

Why do you think that is?

_____
_____
_____
_____

If yes, the book suggests language you could use to create positive reinforcement of your attributes in their minds. Please read this language, and then list the phrases that you find most useful.

_____
_____
_____
_____
_____

Are there other phrases that the suggested language inspires you to create for yourself?

_____
_____
_____
_____

At the end of each description is an "Expect me to…." statement. How true of you is this?

Please circle: True | False | Somewhat true

How might you alter the description or what might you add to it?

_____

_____

_____

_____

_____

_____

Tips

As you think through the tips given in this chapter, please take note of the following encouragement:

> "... Embrace the best in who people say you are. Don't chase the mirage of who you would rather be, for the sake of greater popularity; it will only lead to you disappointing yourself and others. A healthy self-awareness, clearly defined and backed by up action, will not only help you find your place in this world, but will also help you gain the respect and admiration of others."

How might you rewrite the author's paraphrase of The Serenity Prayer if you were to make it specific to the things you are learning about your *evident*, *latent*, and *absent* potential?

"God, grant me the serenity to share the things *I cannot change* about myself (*absent*), courage to ask others to challenge me *to improve the things I can* (*evident* and *latent*), and wisdom to know the difference."

Write your version by replacing the generic statements with specific ones.

_____
_____
_____
_____
_____

Now let's take a look at the more generic tips given in order to help you clearly define yourself to others.

Tip #1: Define yourself before others do.

If you leave a communication gap, it will often get filled with nonsense. In the past, have there been situations where you did not clearly communicate what you had to offer? If so, what was expected of you that should not have been expected of you?

_____
_____
_____
_____
_____

Tip #2: Define what makes you unique.

If you want to be a more interesting communicator, then major on what is distinctive and minor on what is generic. People will listen to you more attentively if you spend less time talking about what is already generally agreed upon and more time on what is different, new, fresh, or unique about what you are saying.

My**Shapes** Journal

Take these generic statements and make them more specific by explaining not simply *what* you like to do, but *how* you like to do it.

"I like to help people."

_____
_____
_____
_____
_____

"I like to encourage people."

_____
_____
_____
_____
_____

"I like to serve people."

_____
_____
_____
_____
_____

Tip #3: Define what success looks like to you.

New vision requires new measurements of success. If you are to build something good with others, how would you measure that success? Again, make it tangible, not abstract. What do you want people to know you can achieve if they allow you to play to your strengths?

___

Tip #4: Define what failure looks like to you.

Equally, do not be afraid to share with them how you might let them down if you are forced to concentrate on your weaknesses. If people trust your motives, they will pivot their expectations.

MyShapes Journal

Challenge

How does this chapter help you understand how to better communicate who you are to others?

_____

_____

_____

_____

Earlier, you wrote how you would like people to describe you to others. Has this changed at all? If so, in what way? Please spend time going into the details.

_____

_____

_____

_____

Now, try to summarize all of this in a short and simple phrase. Imagine you are offering to build something good with someone else and you want to share with them what you have to offer. Keep it to no more than 8-10 words, less if possible. Try to include the two important ingredients: What people should expect of you and what people should not expect of you.

_____

_____

_____

_____

9. The Wisdom of a Fish

How do I share what I need?

Stress

Absent

When you invite others to help you, some people actually make things worse. Why? Because they offer the kind of help that they themselves would want, but do not provide the kind of assistance you might actually need. Can you think of a situation when this has happened?

_____
_____
_____
_____
_____

To harness the strengths of others, there are two things to bear in mind:

1. It is vital that we recognize and admit that we struggle. So what causes you the greatest stress or inner turmoil when trying to build something good with others?

_____
_____
_____
_____

2. We must communicate exactly what we hope to get from them. Has anything caused you to hold back from sharing your need for other people's help? Or have you struggled to find the correct words, correct tone, or correct timing to do this?

_____
_____
_____
_____
_____

Indicators

Stress can come in different forms for different Shapes.

Similar to our demotivators, our stress points can have negative results on our relationships. But, unlike our demotivators, the indicators in this chapter tend to be the ones we create ourselves. They are the result of a personality type operating in isolation. In this section of the book, the author offers a five-part generic description of how each Shape may relate to stress:

1. What causes stress is mentioned in the first sentence. Is this true of you?

   Please circle: Yes | No

2. Read the general description of how this may play out for your Shape. Which parts of this do you relate to?

   _____
   _____
   _____
   _____

3. Read the three italicized words that highlight key triggers for your Shape. Please rate them in order of how true they are of you and then explain where and when you have seen their effects within your own life. If you cannot relate to any of them, please state why.

_____
_____
_____
_____

1st............................
2nd...........................
3rd............................

_____
_____
_____
_____

4. Read the four stress indicators. Please rate them in order of how true they are of you and then explain where and when you have responded this way within your own life. If you cannot relate to any of them, please state why.

_____
_____
_____
_____

Equilibrium

In this section, the book lists four areas of pressure that we can face. The author highlights the importance of addressing each one specifically and realizing the need to combat them differently. Do you feel you are under stress right now in any of the four areas listed below? If so, please list them in order of concern and make note of where that pressure comes from. Is it from someone else or the circumstances you find yourself in? If you do not feel you are suffering from stress in any of these areas, then do not add them to the list.

Please circle: Mental | Physical | Emotional | Spiritual

1st ....

2nd ....

3rd ....

4th ....

A key skill to making yourself better understood is to communicate not just *what* you need from others but *how* you need it. Please take a look at the advice on what to know and share. The aim of this is to give you the words to express yourself as well as the affirmation that doing so is not a bad thing!

Read the description of your Shape's reaction to stress. Is this accurate of you?

Please circle: Yes | No | Somewhat

If yes, why? If no, why not? If somewhat, how might you change or add to the description?

_____

_____

MAKE YOURSELF UNDERSTOOD

_____
_____
_____
_____

Now take a look at the suggested language you could use to share what you really need from others when you collaborate with them. Making yourself better understood in this way will help towards relieving some of the pressure you put yourself under and that others might inadvertently pile on top of you.

First, which ones help you understand something about yourself for the first time?

_____
_____
_____
_____
_____
_____

Secondly, which ones do you think you should use that you aren't already using?

_____
_____
_____
_____
_____
_____

Thirdly, what's missing? What phrases has this chapter helped you create?

_____

_____

_____

_____

_____

Tips

As the author says:

> "The sooner you decide to communicate your needs . . . the sooner you will wonder why you never did it before! However, as much as sharing our burdens is important, we cannot hope that our friends, employers, or family can remove them. . . . Therefore, we must be more proactive when we take care of ourselves and one another."

Take time to read the generic tips and then answer the following questions.

Tip #1: I have made some personal commitments to myself.

Based on the four areas of stress you spent time contemplating above, how do you create equilibrium in each area? If you do not presently make commitments to your own well-being mentally, physically, emotionally, or spiritually, what plans could you put in place to do so?

1. _____

2. _____

3. _____

4. _____

Tip #2: I focus on the climate rather than the weather.

Do you focus on the 'weather' or 'climate' of your emotions, and how might your Shape influence this? What changes, if any, do you need to make when it comes to how you focus on your problems?

_____
_____
_____
_____
_____

Tip #3: I've learned to think about how I feel and vice versa.

Are you a thinker or a feeler? How might you balance this out in the way the book suggests you do?

_____
_____
_____
_____
_____

Tip #4: I take a little time out to enjoy the fruits of any success.

Don't presume that people will want to celebrate success the way you most enjoy it. Instead, take time to list the ways in which you like to celebrate success, and think through how you can share that with people.

_____
_____

MyShapes Journal

_____
_____
_____
_____

Tip #5: Recognize that the grass is often tinged with yellow on the other side.

Prompted by the proverb used in the book, "Don't throw away the water you are carrying because you see a mirage," do you also need to balance your desires for the future by proactively appreciating what you already have?

Yes | No | Maybe

If yes, how might you do this? If no, is that because you already do? If maybe, what is your thinking behind your answer?

_____
_____
_____
_____
_____
_____

Challenge

How does this chapter help you better understand your reaction to stress?

_____
_____

MAKE YOURSELF UNDERSTOOD

_____
_____
_____
_____
_____

Draw a picture or diagram to illustrate how your family, friends, and colleagues can best help you cope with the stresses and strains in your life.

Now share it with them. Maybe you could do that by posting it on your social media or putting it up on your bedroom door. One couple who did The Shapes Test™ has posted key points on their bathroom mirror so that they are reminded of each other's needs every day.

10. Social Reality

How do I share what I have to give?

Influence

Math

As the author says, *"It's no good having something good to offer if no one knows it's being offered!"*

In this chapter, an equation is used to explain the potential of any group of people who use their evident potential in order to bring out each other's *latent* potential. We are also warned that if we do not harness the benefits of a many-to-many concept in order to bring something good into our world, others may use this dynamic to bring something bad.

> " . . . In every generation I see a clear obstacle in the form of poor communication, both internally and externally. . . . Internally, when recognizing the latent potential in a friend, neighbor, or colleague and considering the idea of offering to help them, do you ask, 'Who do I think I am to suggest this?' Or perhaps, 'What makes me so great?' Might you talk yourself out of helping people in this way?"

What causes you to doubt yourself or hold back from offering your evident potential, such as your wisdom, talent, or insight? Do you talk yourself out of helping people?

Yes | No | Sometimes

MAKE YOURSELF UNDERSTOOD

When was the last time you held back in this way and what was the reason you gave yourself?

_____
_____
_____
_____
_____

The different personalities complicate this even further, as our well-intentioned positivity can be perceived poorly due to the various ways Shapes communicate their thoughts and feelings. If we don't do a good job of making ourselves understood, each Shape has the ability to come across badly. Take a look at the descriptions listed for your Shape in the book.

Can you relate to the potential problem that your Shape may encounter if you 'promote' yourself by offering your *evident* potential to help others become the best they can be?

Please circle: Yes | No | Maybe, as I suspect people think this about me

Could this disable you in any way, and if so how?

_____
_____
_____
_____
_____

Numbers

Have you experienced what the author refers to as 'Social Reality'?

Please circle: Yes | No | Possibly

If people have others alongside them in order to help them do what needs to be done, goal-setting transitions from a negative to a positive tool. Therefore, please think through a goal you might have for the following types of people in your life. Specifically ask yourself, "What is the latent potential I see in them that I can help them discover or improve upon?"

A Friend:

    Name - _____

    Their Potential -

_____
_____
_____
_____

A Colleague:

    Name - _____

    Their Potential -

_____
_____
_____
_____

A Family Member:

    Name - _____

    Their Potential -

_____
_____
_____
_____

Language

What The Shapes Test™ hopes to supply more than anything else is language. In particular, language that helps you express yourself in a way that avoids the problem of people misunderstanding or misinterpreting your offer of help. In this section of the book, the author offers a five-part generic description of how each Shape may best share what they want to offer:

1. The first part is what you may want to offer people. Is this accurate?

    Please circle: Yes | No

    Why?

    _____
    _____
    _____
    _____
    _____

MyShapes Journal

2. Is the "You might say..." statement true of you?

   Please circle: Yes | No | Somewhat

   Why?

   _____
   _____
   _____
   _____

3. Which parts of the general description are most accurate and useful when offering your help?

   _____
   _____
   _____
   _____

4. Do you relate to the quote listed in your Shape's description?

   Please circle: Yes | No | Somewhat

   Why?

   _____
   _____
   _____
   _____

5. Of the seven phrases you might want to use, please rate them in order of how true they are of you and then make note of your reasons for this.

   1st _____

   2nd _____

   3rd _____

   4th _____

   5th _____

   6th _____

   7th _____

How does this chapter help you better understand your ability to influence others?

_____

_____

_____

_____

_____

Of the tips given in this chapter, which one is the most helpful?

_____

_____

_____

_____

_____

On a scale of 1 to 10, how willing are you to commit to building something good with someone else?

1 | 2 | 3 | 4 | 5 | 6 | 7 | 8 | 9 | 10

Tips

Learning how to clearly and concisely communicate what you want to give, makes your offer of help more likely to succeed! Of course, positive language driven by a genuine love for people covers a multitude of communication sins. Perhaps more than ever before, people value someone who will bring a positive influence into their lives.

So, take time to read the following tips and then answer the questions.

Tip #1: Don't throw your pearls to the pigs.

As much as you are encouraged to offer your help to others, never offer it to those who have clearly expressed that they don't want it. With this in mind, how likely are you to recognize when people are unwilling to learn from you?

_____
_____
_____
_____

What signs do you need to take note of earlier rather than later?

_____
_____
_____
_____

MAKE YOURSELF UNDERSTOOD

Tip #2: Listen to what they really need.

What can you do to improve your listening skills?

_____
_____
_____
_____

Using the same people you made note of earlier, list the questions you might want to ask in order to clarify how they might want to receive your offer of help.

A Friend:

    Name - _____   Their Shape - _____

    Their Potential -

_____
_____
_____
_____

A Colleague:

    Name - _____   Their Shape - _____

    Their Potential -

_____
_____
_____

My**Shapes** Journal

_____
_____

A Family Member:

    Name - _____ Their Shape - _____

    What questions do you have for them?

_____
_____
_____
_____

Tip #3: Build on joint objectives.

Once you have listened to people, find a joint objective. Never try to force someone into a goal that they do not believe in, nor try to help someone with a goal you do not believe that they can achieve. Instead, find something you can honestly commit to and make a note of it. You might want to clearly outline the levels of encouragement and criticism you are both willing to give and receive.

Here's a space to make note of any conversations you have around this matter.

A Friend:

    The goal - _____

A Colleague:

    The goal - _____

A Family Member:

    The goal - _____

Tip #4: Build on shared credit.

The author shares a great rule he heard when partnering with someone: If we succeed, "You did it." If we do okay, "We did it." If we fail, "I did it."

Where have you accepted credit without properly giving it?

_____
_____
_____
_____
_____

What might you do differently in the future?

_____
_____
_____
_____
_____

Tip #5: The more specific it is . . . the more dynamic it will be.

Take note of the suggestions the author gives when it comes to words of encouragement regarding the difference between specific and generic communication.

MyShapes Journal

Rather than using general words to encourage your friend, what specific words could you use?

_____
_____
_____
_____

Rather than using general words to encourage your colleague, what specific words could you use?

_____
_____
_____
_____

Rather than using general words to encourage your family member, what specific words could you use?

_____
_____
_____
_____

Tip #7: Make a commitment and then stick to it.

How long are you prepared to help build something good with your friend?

With your colleague?

With your family member?

What are the signs that will help you know you have gone as far as you can or need to go?

_____
_____
_____
_____

Challenge

Hopefully by now, you have a good sense of understanding yourself, understanding others, and how better to make yourself understood. The question remains, what will you do with this newfound awareness?

It is a fact that you are more likely to offer yourself if you have someone to encourage you along the way. So, the challenge is to go find that person, tell them your plan, and ask them to help you to take the steps you need to take by offering encouragement and criticism when they feel you need it.

1. Decide who you want that person to be and ask them to help you.
2. Create your plan using the outline on the following page.
3. Give them permission to encourage and criticize you.

My Plan

We hope that this journal has been of some help in the *receiving, discerning,* and *repeating* process that helps turn the contents of the book into greater Relational Intelligence. We are excited that you are determined to build something good with others. Below is a very simple outline to help you build your MyShapes Plan.

What I want to build:

_____
_____
_____
_____
_____

Who I want to build it with:

_____
_____
_____
_____
_____

The strengths I have to give and how I can best give them:

_____
_____
_____
_____
_____

The weaknesses I need to manage:

_____
_____
_____
_____

The help I need and how I need it to be given to me:

_____
_____
_____
_____

The timeline I need:

_____
_____
_____
_____
_____

My next step:

_____
_____
_____
_____

My**Shapes** Journal

Connect with the Author

Paul Clayton Gibbs is the creator of The Shapes Test. He and his wife, The Foxy Lynn, have two adult sons and have recently become the proud grandparents of two beautiful girls. Originally from Manchester, England, the Gibbs family moved to the USA in 2005.

Founder of The Pais Movement, a faith-based organization that creates workable symmetry between organizations, Paul seeks to help people build something good together. Paul has written several books and spends a significant amount of time traveling throughout the world speaking at conferences, businesses, churches and other acting as a consultant for various networks. His primary topics are leadership development, mentoring and missional living. He is the CEO of The Masterclass Suite and is also the creator of various training 'templates' aimed at 'Mobilizing the many, not just the few.'

Paul enjoys swimming, sailing, bodyboarding, skiing, snowboarding, mountain biking and is a lifelong Manchester United fan!

instagram paulcgibbs
facebook paulclaytongibbs
instagram theshapestest
facebook theshapestest

Made in the USA
Monee, IL
05 May 2024